HE DIED, WA

GW01393112

We read in the First E
that:

> 'Christ died for
> Scriptures, and that He was buried, and that
> He rose again the third day according to the
> Scriptures, and that He was seen by Cephas,
> then by the twelve. After that He was seen by
> over five hundred brethren at once, of whom
> the greater part remain to the present, but
> some have fallen asleep. After that He was seen
> by James, then by all the apostles. Then last of
> all He was seen by me also, as by one born out
> of due time'   (15:3–8)

Paul—a Pharisee and contemporary of the disciples and
apostles of Jesus—sought out, after his own Damascus
Road conversion to Christianity (Acts 9), the full facts
surrounding the third day resurrection of Jesus the
Nazarene which has astonished the world. He was, in
the providence of God, a man of letters and a student of
the Old Testament Scriptures. Thus his monologue in
1 Corinthians 15 asserting and defending the historical
and prophetic fulfilment of Jesus Christ's resurrection
also notes that there were surviving eyewitnesses in his
day totalling about 520 persons.

The four New Testament Gospels that will be read all over the world on Easter Sunday, together with millions of sermons and expositions on this vital topic, will (helped by the Holy Spirit) bring to hearts and minds the truth about the resurrection. When that happens people will hear, believe and trust in Christ for salvation (*cf.* Acts 17:32).

> **The Easter story is about life not death**

The Easter story is about life not death. This means that everything depends on whether or not Jesus Christ rose from the dead on the third day. What are the facts?

1. The Jews, Romans and Christians all agree that Jesus Christ was dead when taken from the Cross.

2. That He was buried in a new tomb.

3. That on the third day His body was missing.

4. That Jesus' body was not removed by Jews, Romans or Jesus' disciples, so where had it gone?

5. When the women arrived at the tomb early on Sunday morning (to continue the burial preparations on Jesus' body) they found the stone rolled away. They did not come to the wrong tomb because the Bible tells us that they took diligent note of where it was and how to get there (Matthew 27:61; Luke 23:53–55; John 19:40-42).

6. That on the same morning, the risen Saviour Jesus Christ appeared to His first witness, Mary Magdalene (John 20:14, 18).

7. That the Jewish and Roman officers could not recover the missing body.

8. The risen Saviour appeared at least twelve times to various individuals and groups of disciples over a forty-day period before He ascended into heaven to the Father (see the table on page 23).

9. The Apostles and disciples of Jesus believed in His resurrection and were willing to die proclaiming it to be true and the fulfilment of Old Testament prophecy (Acts 2:30–35, etc.).

I have summarised the historical evidence above that comes from the New Testament and can be found in Matthew 28, Mark 16, Luke 24 and in John 20. All four Gospels give the record of Christ's death, burial and resurrection.

His crucifixion

Crucifixion was the most terrible torture ever devised. The word comes from the Latin *crucifigere* which means 'to fix to a cross'. The method was invented by the ancient Phoenicians and was made even more brutal by the Romans, who added a cross member to the initial vertical stake. Crucifixion was an everyday event in the Roman Empire, but it was not common in Palestine when Pilate was governor. It was a barbaric mode of capital punishment as it allowed no mercy but rather was designed to inflict maximum pain and suffering. The Romans used it as a punishment for slaves, but their own citizens were exempt. The Emperor Constantine I abolished it in AD 315.

This method of Christ's death was of man's devising, but it was also in fulfilment of Old Testament prophecy. This is seen from Psalm 22, where we read *'all My bones are out of joint'* (v. 14) and *'they pierced My hands and My feet'* (v. 16). This psalm reads like a contemporary eyewitness narrative, yet it was part of the Jewish Old Testament canon written around a thousand years before the time of Christ (compare Matthew 27:39, 43–46). Our Saviour was certified dead after the Roman soldier used a spear to puncture the pericardium (the membrane that encloses the heart) *'and immediately blood and water came out'* (John 19:34). On the cross, breathing would have been very difficult indeed, and the heart of Jesus had to work harder and would eventually have produced 'water', that is, a clear fluid containing no red or white blood cells.

Psalm 22 reads like a contemporary eyewitness narrative

His death

In the plan and purpose of God, Jesus Christ's death achieved atonement for sin and reconciliation between God and fallen humankind so that all sinners who believe find peace with God. *'Jesus our Lord … was delivered up for our trespasses and raised for our justification'* (Romans 4:24–25, AV); *'Christ also has loved us and given Himself for us, an offering and a sacrifice to God for a sweet-smelling aroma'* (Ephesians 5:2; see also 2:14–18). Calvin points out that:

> *'Sin is the cause of enmity between God and us; and, until it is removed, we shall not be restored to the Divine favour. It has been blotted out by the death of Christ, in which He offered himself to the Father as an expiatory victim.'* [1]

The death of Christ reconciled sinners to God: *'You, who once were alienated and enemies in your mind by wicked works, yet now He has reconciled in the body of His flesh through death, to present you holy, and blameless, and above reproach in His sight'* (Colossians 1:21–22). These verses speak of man's estrangement from Jesus Christ his Creator (John 1:2–3; Colossians 1:16); so when Paul talks of being reconciled to God he is preaching the gospel. Reconciliation means a restoration of friendship between God and us. It was

> **Reconciliation means a restoration of friendship between God and us**

the Father who sent the Son to Calvary; there the Son was judged, sentenced and punished on our account to establish peace. The ultimate aim of atoning reconciliation is the removal of God's estrangement and the presentation of believers as *'holy, and blameless, and above reproach in His sight'* (see also Romans 3:25; 1 John 2:1–2).

His burial

The Gospels give us the facts regarding Christ's burial. His body was placed in a new tomb owned by a rich man called Joseph of Arimathea. Here Christ lay until the third day. A guard was placed by the Romans at the tomb with the agreement of the Jewish hierarchy so that the body would not be stolen. The significance of His burial is threefold:

- It was the fulfilment of Old Testament prophecy. In Psalm 16:10 King David said, *'For You will not leave my soul in Sheol, nor will You allow Your Holy One to see corruption'*, yet David himself was buried but did not rise from the dead. These words were quoted by the apostle Peter on the Day of Pentecost (Acts 2:31) as proof that Jesus Christ was the promised and awaited Messiah of the Jews.

- It proves that the Roman soldiers had certified Jesus as dead when they took Him down from the cross. They were used to this procedure and were sure that He was deceased (Mark 15:44).

- Jesus's followers took careful note of the location of the tomb where He was buried (Luke 23:55). It was definitely that tomb they visited early on the Sunday morning—however, it was empty; thus they became eyewitnesses to Christ's resurrection.

His resurrection

> *'The resurrection is the most important article of our faith'*　　　　　　(John Calvin)

The resurrection receives special attention in all four Gospels because it lies at the very heart of the Christian faith; take it away and all that is left of Christianity is another religion whose founder is dead and buried and whose teachings can be superseded in the years to come. However, all honest readers of the Bible must agree that Scripture teaches without reservation or contradiction that Jesus Christ rose from the dead on the third day, and that that day was the first day of the week (Sunday).

When the women arrived at the tomb early on Sunday morning to continue their burial preparations on Jesus' body, expecting to find the corpse where they had laid it two days before, they found the stone rolled away and the tomb vacant (Luke 24:1–3). The Bible states that an angel of God had removed the stone

(Matthew 28:2). A short time later, the risen Saviour appeared to Mary Magdalene.

Christians believe that their faith is rooted in historical fact and not fiction. The Bible proclaims the fact of Christ's resurrection, but it does not attempt to describe the process. It simply tells us what happened and expects us to believe it. Those who reject the truth of Christ's resurrection reject the testimony of the holy Scriptures, seeing it as unreliable, and they charge its writers (the apostles and prophets) with fraud and deceit. One thing is clear, however:

> **Christians believe that their faith is rooted in historical fact and not fiction**

'Christ redeemed the whole person, and thus the consummation of redemption must involve the redemption of the body (Romans 8:23; cf. Ephesians 1:14). It is in the integrity of personal life, reconstructed by resurrection, that the saints will enter into and eternally enjoy the inheritance incorruptible, undefiled, and unfading'.[2]

Death defeated

Resurrection is the triumph of Jesus Christ over *'the last enemy'*, death (1 Corinthians 15:26). Because of this, believers can be confident that on the last day they will rise as He did. Christ has defeated Satan, who had the power of death. This power was taken from Satan at the cross (Colossians 2:14; Hebrews 2:14–15).

When the resurrection day arrives, believers will be given bodies like that of the risen Saviour; these new bodies will be perfect, fitted for a spiritual existence and with the power of an endless life (1 Corinthians 15:50–55). Here is the solution to death and its humiliation. Those who believe the words *'I am the resurrection and the life'* (John 11:25) will share in Christ's everlasting victory. As A. W. Pink puts it:

> *'Then shall be fulfilled that mystical word, "I say to you that many will come from east and west, and sit down with Abraham, Isaac, and Jacob in the kingdom of heaven" (Matthew 8:11). As the Lord Jesus declared, "I lay down my life for the sheep. And other sheep I have which are not of this fold; them also I must bring, and they will hear My voice; and there will be one flock and one shepherd" (John 10:15–16). Then it shall be that Christ will "gather together in one the children of God who were scattered abroad" (John 11:52)— not only among all nations, but through all dispensations.'* [3]

Christians must oppose all attempts to deny, invalidate or rewrite the resurrection accounts as found in the four Gospels. Such attempts are common today, with, for example, increasing amounts of literature being produced by Islamic sources to discredit the four historical accounts in the Gospels. One such effort is centred on the New Testament phrase *'the sign of the prophet Jonah'* (this saying is exploited by Muslims to deny the death and resurrection of our Saviour).[4]

The Quran

The resurrection of Jesus is not regarded as true by Islam, which claims that Jesus did not die on the cross and that Judas (or another) was substituted in His place. Muslims believe that there was no atoning death by Jesus of Nazareth, the Messiah of the Jews. Rather, the planned death of Jesus was thwarted when another person was crucified in His place:

> *'They did not kill him, nor did they crucify him, but it only seemed to them [as if it had been so]'*

> (Sura 4:157)

Muslims are therefore taught that whoever died on the cross it was *not* Jesus Christ: 'a substitute was made to look like Jesus and was crucified in his place while Jesus was taken straight up to heaven (without dying).'[5] This idea has no historical substance or theological credibility. No secular historian doubts that Jesus was a historical person and that He was crucified and buried. So this assertion that it was not

Jesus is without historical foundation. Some Muslims believe in the authority of a book called the *Gospel of Barnabas*, stating it to have been written by one of the disciples of Jesus. This book purports that it was Judas Iscariot who was crucified in the place of Jesus:

> '*The holy angels came and took Jesus out by the window that looketh toward the south. They bare him and placed him in the third heaven ... Judas was so changed in speech and in face to be like Jesus that we believed him to be Jesus.*'[6]

Because Islam believes that there was no death of Jesus at Calvary but instead transference into a 'third' heaven, there can be no bodily resurrection of Jesus in Islamic theology. This is contrary to the Scriptures. The Apostle Peter spoke about Jesus Christ's resurrection and its implications, not only at Pentecost in Acts 2 but again to the 'Rulers of the people and elders of Israel' in Acts 4:

The Apostle Peter spoke about Jesus Christ's resurrection and its implications

> '*Then Peter, filled with the Holy Spirit, said to them, "...let it be known to you all, and to all the people of Israel, that ... Jesus Christ of Nazareth, whom you crucified ... God raised from the dead ... This is the 'stone which was rejected by you builders, which has become the*

chief cornerstone.' Nor is there salvation in any other, for there is no other name under heaven given among men by which we must be saved.'"

(vv. 8a, 10–12)

Because Islam believes that Jesus did not die on a cross but was transferred into a 'third' heaven there can be no resurrection of Jesus on the third day from the dead. This denial of the death and third day resurrection of Jesus by Islam strikes at the very heart of the Gospel and is aimed at the foundation of the Church. This makes the two religions incompatible.

What do the death, burial and resurrection of Jesus Christ mean for us?

1. Jesus Christ's resurrection proves his deity. Paul tells us so in Romans chapter one. Jesus was 'declared *to be* the Son of God with power according to the Spirit of holiness, by the resurrection from the dead' (v. 4).

2. God accepted His Son's death as an atoning sacrifice and a ransom for sins, bringing forgiveness through the blood of the cross. Jesus Christ's spotless sinless life and reconciling death were good enough to pay the price of sin: 'he only (alone) could unlock the gate of heaven and let us in'. Christians are accepted in the Beloved and can approach God through the blood of the cross. This means they

can stand before a holy God and call Him *'Abba, Father'* (Galatians 4:6).

3. Peace *with* God through our Lord Jesus Christ, because *'He was raised for our justification'* (Romans 4:25). The justifying peace *with* God is ours resulting in the peace *of* God in the soul. If He is still dead then we are still unsaved, still lost, still helpless in our sins for *'all our righteousnesses are like filthy rags'* in God's sight (Isaiah 64:6).

4. It brings joy to the believer: *'So they went out quickly from the tomb with fear and great joy...'* (Matthew 28:8–9). This is true joy, never to be forgotten, lost or denied as believers abide in Christ Jesus their Lord and Saviour. It is always present in those who believe.

5. Resurrection means that believers need not fear death any more. He gives peace and assurance by His [Holy] Spirit. He supplies hope by the promises given to all who have trusted Him for forgiveness and cleansing in the blood of the Lamb. As believers we are not to fear death but rejoice in the promise of entering into His presence at death and rising at the Last Day to become like Him (Philippians 3:20–21; 1 John 3:1–2). Death has been conquered by Jesus Christ, and because we are in Him by faith we have the victory: *'O death,*

where is thy sting? O grave, where is thy victory?'
(1 Corinthians 15:55ff, AV).

6. We can be Jesus' witnesses, telling the gospel story to others *'with fear and great joy'* (Matthew 28:8). The first thing the risen Jesus commanded was the proclamation to others that He was alive (Matthew 28:7, 16–20). What a calling! What a privilege we have to gossip the gospel like the early disciples, telling our neighbours that He is 'risen indeed'!

7. It changed the day of worship. The days of the week are now ordered from the day Jesus arose from the dead. This changed the Sabbath day from the last day of the week (Saturday) to the first (Sunday) and it had a mighty impact on the church and the world.

8. The Holy Spirit was sent in power on the Apostles and believers forty days after Christ ascended to heaven. Now the plan of salvation was on course and the world could be evangelised.

9. The resurrection of Jesus secures the authority of preaching, bringing life to the spiritually dead.

The resurrection means that Jesus is alive, not just in our memories or retained in the church's historic dogma and

Jesus is alive ... really and truly and literally

theology, but really and truly and literally. Ours is not a dead religion nor a blind faith but one based on historical fact and the empty tomb: *'He is not here; for He is risen ... Come, see the place where the Lord lay'* (Matthew 28:6). His cold bed was empty and the women went off to, *'tell His disciples that He is risen from the dead'* (v.7). Their example should be ours too.

It is needful that the Story be told still

The Apostles gave the third day resurrection of Jesus Christ from the dead a central place in their messaging and they preached victory over death. They believed that Jesus came back from the dead and that He lives in heaven now to save us. That is *still* the message of hope for us all: *'He is also able to save to the uttermost those who come to God through Him, since He always lives to make intercession for them'* (Hebrews 7:25).

The Acts

The resurrection was the central theme of the preaching of the Apostles recorded for us by Dr Luke. They are not the inventions of that historian (author of the third Gospel) but accounts of speeches actually made by the Apostles and therefore valuable and independent sources on the history of the resurrection and the content of their preaching in the early church (from

Luke, a Greek Christian). The speeches recorded by Luke are faithful records containing a unity in reality and theology.[7]

We are then to trust the inspired Scripture which sets before us the true story of the resurrection and the apostolic passion to make it known.[8] The centrality of the resurrection in the preaching in Acts is clearly seen by observant readers: in three main passages Luke relates that the early church laid stress on the resurrection in debate with the Jews:

(i) Acts 23:7ff refers to the well-known dispute between the Pharisees and the Sadducees, the latter denying it. The apostles preached *in Jesus the resurrection from the dead* (Acts 4:2). The main opposition came from the Sadducees (Acts 4:1ff), but the Pharisees (or some of them) were less ready to condemn the Christians unheard (Acts 5:33ff). Representatives of both parties, however, were converted to the faith (Acts 6:7).

(ii) Acts 24:15–21 shows that Paul (a Pharisee) became a Christian as there was nothing inconsistent about a claim that 'Christian belief was in effect the fulfilment of Judaism' (Acts 28:20).

(iii) To the Greeks and the early Gnostics the idea of bodily resurrection was strange and incompatible with their own philosophical ideas (Acts 17:31–32).

Paul, who believed the Scriptures, rejected Greek ideas and argued for the proof and legitimacy of Old Testament prophecy by declaring to his listeners the implications of the resurrection of Jesus on the third day, and some believed (Acts 17:31–34). To refuse the resurrection as true is to deny the faith and destroy hope (2 Timothy 2:17b–18).

1 Corinthians 15

In 1 Corinthians 15 the truth of the resurrection of Jesus Christ is summarised and expounded carefully with the aid of the Holy Spirit. Paul was writing to encourage faith and bring hope because the idea of 'resurrection' is against all logic and previous human experience. Paul also wants the churches to proclaim the physical resurrection with exciting, persevering zeal (v. 58).

> **Without the historic reality of the resurrection faith in Christ is in vain**

We need to grasp that without the historic reality of the resurrection faith in Christ is in vain for, *'If Christ be not risen, then is our preaching vain, and your faith is also vain [empty]'* (15:13–14, AV). We should take heed to his words because faith has no benefit if Jesus is still in the tomb: *'...what advantage is it to me? If the dead do not rise, "Let us eat and drink, for tomorrow we die!"'* (v. 32b). Paul's aim in writing was to correct those in error on this very important subject and *also* to encourage evangelism.

People need to hear in order to believe, and telling is informing. Let us speak of the resurrection story and the hope that Christians have through Christ risen from the dead. Let us also remember Paul's application:

'Therefore, my beloved brethren, be steadfast, immovable, always abounding in the work of the Lord, knowing that your labour is not in vain in the Lord' (v. 58).

> **People need to hear in order to believe, and telling is informing**

Exponential growth

It is obvious that the resurrection story was central to the exponential growth of the church as it met the need in the hearts of people for hope in the afterlife. This is therefore the story we should tell more often in our contemporary evangelism: 'He is not here, He has risen indeed!' This messaging is the reason for Paul's monograph and his short but practical application (v. 58). This loving exclamation is to remind them of the implications of what he has just written and he adds a practical application, viz., to be unwavering, unbending and always abounding in gospel work. He wants the Corinthians to take to heart the significance of the resurrection and to be active in Easter Story evangelism; not only at Easter *but in all their outreach.*

We are encouraged here by Paul to tell the story of full redemption as he told it to the Corinthians. He was calling them to show zeal and a consistent approach that is *steadfast* (Gk. *hedraioi* = 'be strong'). This is not about self-assertiveness but an upholding of gospel hope and the witness of faith. He adds, *'be immovable'* (i.e. *'Let nothing move you'*). It is a similar word to 'steadfast', so there is a double thrust towards constancy of purpose. Remember to be *always abounding*, which suggests a pouring out of effort and an increase of service by going the second mile (Matthew 5:41). Our usefulness in the Lord's kingdom depends on how much we are obedient and self-sacrificing. We are to trust God at all times and let our love for the Lord Jesus keep us *'redeeming the time'* in evil days (Ephesians 5:16).

This loving encouragement is to refresh hope, *'knowing that your labour is not in vain in the Lord'*. What we do for Jesus is not in vain, nor is it empty as some may feel or say. To *'labour'* for Jesus is not wasted (Gk. *kopos*, i.e. with effort, and energy, and is used describing 'weariness' and 'fatigue'). In fact we will in the future wish we had given Him

To 'labour' for Jesus is not wasted

more! What we do is to be done 'as unto Him' (Colossians 3:23), not for self but for *His* glory and His kingdom. This is achieved when we take up our cross and follow Him. We should ask ourselves, 'Do I labour in His harvest fields with self-sacrifice and hope?' and, am I 'always abounding in the work of the Lord'?

Paul now encourages them to tell the story of full redemption. In 1 Corinthians 15:51–52a) he preaches that a momentous change is coming and all things will alter for the better: *'We shall not all sleep, but we shall all be changed—in a moment, in the twinkling of an eye, at the last trumpet.'*[9] The phrase, *'We shall all be changed'* speaks of the end of time and the resurrection day which will come, *'in a moment'* (Gk, *atomo*; that is, a *time* so short as to be incapable of further division). This disagrees with the evolutionary theory which believes that it takes long, long ages for corporeal flesh to change from one form into another.

We are, however, to tell others that there is hope of eternal life offered in Jesus Christ before the Second Coming and the Day of Judgement dawns. In a millisecond—*'in the twinkling of an eye we shall all be changed'*! This means that there will be no time left to change our minds, or repent, or say sorry!

There will be no time left to change our minds

When transformed by the power of God unto Jesus Christ's risen likeness we shall be unable to sin because His holiness (impeccability) will be shared with us.[10]

On earth the incarnate God-man Christ Jesus was 'not able to sin', and all the saints, being wholly transformed and conformed at the resurrection, will be as He is, which secures for eternity a holy re-creation and new humanity:[11]

> '...our citizenship is in heaven, from which we also eagerly wait for the Saviour, the Lord Jesus Christ, who will **transform** our lowly body that it may be **conformed** to His glorious body, according to the working by which He is able even to subdue all things to Himself.'
>
> (Philippians 3:20–21)

Conclusion

The Christian faith is based on history not on myth, and on facts not fiction. John tells us (John 20) that on the resurrection morning the linen bandages which were wrapped around Jesus' corpse by Joseph of Arimathea and Nicodemus were lying unfilled for all who entered the sarcophagus to see—minus a body! If the body had been stolen or Jesus had revived in the cool of the tomb the grave cloths would have been removed or discarded. But not so; rather, they were lying just where the carcase was placed but without a body wrapped in them (John 20:6–8; Luke 24:12).

> The Christian faith is based on history not on myth, and on facts not fiction

The believer's hope depends on whether or not Jesus Christ rose from the dead on the third day, and the believer's trust is in the One who said:

> *'I am the resurrection and the life. He who believes in Me, though he may die, he shall live. And whoever lives and believes in Me shall never die. Do you believe this?'*
>
> (John 11:25–26)

A harmony of Jesus Christ's resurrection appearances during the forty days until His ascension (Acts 1:3)

No.	Person/people	NT Text	AD 30 & place
1	To Mary Magdalene	Matt. 28:9 Mark 16:9 Luke 24:1–11 John 20:14–16	Jerusalem on the first day of the week (the Lord's day)
2	To the group of women who visited the sepulchre	Matt. 28:9 Mark 16:1–8	Jerusalem on the first day of the week
3	To apostle Simon Peter (Cephas) alone	Luke 24:34 (12) 1 Cor. 15:5a	Jerusalem on the first day of the week
4	The two disciples on the Emmaus road (one was Cleopas)	Luke 24:13–31	Jerusalem on the first day of the week
5	The apostles except Thomas	John 20:19 Luke 24:36–49 Mark 16:14ff	Jerusalem on the first day of the week
6	The apostles and Thomas (a week later)	John 20: 26, 29	Jerusalem on the second Lord's day (Sunday)
7	The seven by Sea of Tiberius (Galilee)	John 21:1–23	Galilee
8	The eleven disciples on a mountain in Galilee	Matt. 28:16–20 1 Cor. 15:5b	Mountain in Galilee
9	To above 500 brothers at the same time	1 Cor. 15:6	Galilee
10	James Jesus' brother	1 Cor. 15:7a	Unknown
11	To the eleven with others on the ascension day	Acts 1:2-9 Mark 16:19f Luke 24:51 1 Cor. 15:7b	Mount Olivet
12	To Paul 'as one born out of due time'	Acts 9:3–6 1 Cor. 15: 8	Damascus Road

Endnotes

1. John Calvin on Ephesians 2:16, *Commentary* in *John Calvin Collection* (CD_Rom; Christian Library series; Rio, WI: AGES Library, 2007).

2. John Murray, *Collected Writings*, Vol. 2 (The Banner of Truth Trust, Edinburgh, 1977), p. 412.

3. A W Pink, *An Exposition of Hebrews* (Baker Book House, Michigan, 1979), p. 891.

4. See my, *The Real Lord's Prayer* and *Engaging with Islam*, Day One Publications.

5. Patrick Sookhdeo, *Is the Muslim Isa the Biblical Jesus?* (Isaac Publishing, McLean, VA, 2012), p. 8.

6. The *Gospel of Barnabas*, Aisha Bawany ed., (Ashram Publications, Karachi, 1976) in Riddell, Peter G & Peter Cotterell, *Islam in Conflict: past, present and future* (IVP, Leicester, 2003, pp. 78–80).

7. Luke probably completed the third Gospel during Paul's first imprisonment in Rome (61-62 AD). Since the sequel to Luke, the Book of Acts, does not record either Peter's death, Paul's death, or even the fall of Jerusalem (in the face of Jesus' clear prediction of it in Luke 21:6, 20). It is most likely written in the early sixties.

8. Liberal theology has rejected the Lucan record as other than the apostles' beliefs.

9. In this context 'sleep' is a euphemism for death and equivalent to 'die': we shall not all die.

10. It means 'not liable to sin' and comes from the Latin word *impeccabilis*.

11. For the impeccability of Jesus Christ and its implications for our redemption, see my, *The Real Lord's Prayer* (Day One Publications, 2012), pp. 73–78.